broken
symmetry

broken
symmetry

Jack Ridl

Wayne State University Press Detroit

ISBN-13: 978-0-8143-3322-8   ISBN-10: 0-8143-3322-2

Library of Congress Cataloging-in-Publication Data

Ridl, Jack.
Broken symmetry : poems / Jack Ridl.
p. cm. – (Made in Michigan writers series)
ISBN 0-8143-3322-2 (pbk. : alk. paper)
I. Title. II. Series.
PS3568.I3593B76 2006
811'.54—dc22
2005035885

∞

michigan council for
arts and cultural affairs

This book is supported by the Michigan Council for Arts and Cultural Affairs.

Designed and typeset by Maya Rhodes
Composed in Horley Old Style MT and News Gothic

For Meridith and for Julie, love in every line.

Contents

Broken Symmetry   1

II. Quantum Theory

III. Differential Equations

Broken Symmetry

Angels never have to worry
about their wings: lose a feather here
or there, a new perfection floats down
across the landscape, catching itself
on its cousin the tree branch, landing
on its second cousin the leaf, or even
along its third cousin twice removed,
the blacktop highway. There is so much
symmetry that in the mirror your left
side resembles your left side even though
it's never quite the same as your
right. Go deeper. All the cells split
into identical ice dancers, all
the electrons spin the same bacchanal.
Only the broken reveals, gives
the universe its chance at being
interesting, says a door is not
an elephant, the moon is not a
salad fork. So break the bread
in two, drink half the glass of wine,
slice the baby down the middle, cut
the corner, divide the time. Tonight
the moon will once again reflect the sun's
monotonous dazzle, and the old light
making its dumb way to us will break
our symmetry of coming home,
of passing on the street.

I
Fractals

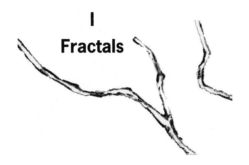

The History of the Pencil

Even as you sit staring at the light
on the new computer that came with speakers
and disks that hold golf games, soundtracks
from the movies of the forties and a way to rhyme
every word except those stubborn loners silver,
purple, and orange, you have to wonder
how this most elemental of juxtapositions,
this marriage that few families would allow,
this wedding of wood and lead, wandered
into some pause in the daydreams
of whom. Even Thoreau, that son
of the pencil-making family who recorded
every move of a leaf, who listed each essential
object for a twelve-day trek into the woods
of Maine—"Matches; soap, two pieces; old
newspapers, three; and blanket, seven feet long"—
neglected to note his pencil. Imagine, held
by the hand of the keeper of Walden
as he, in all his assured solitude, attended
to everything in his burrowing but you,
the scribbler's one essential companion.
Wouldn't you feel much like the friend
who has been there all along, who leaves
quietly out the back door when the famous
come to call, or the good dog who stays
loyal day after abandoned day, or the name,
changed to something more alluring,
that sits and wonders why you are walking away?

"I am a pencil," said Toulouse-Lautrec
to one of the rouged and rowdy-legged dancers
he let become a gray line kicking high
over his lonely head in the dance hall.
Even Leonardo, whose mind would never let
anything escape from the possibility of being better,
wrote those mad, mirror-written obsessions,
his maimed right hand dangling
like a sash, and sketched his own hand
sketching, without ever thinking
that the tedious brush could give way
to something humbler, more subservient.
Did it never enter the mind of some poor
hunter-gatherer, who surely heard the tunes
of the very beasts and berries he searched for,
"I'd like to keep what I'll likely forget. Maybe
if I . . ." Was it there that his mind opened
into the first existential blank? And when
he told her and all his cave companions
what he'd like to be able to do, did they each
just nod and go back to picking out
what had gathered in their hair throughout the day?
So now, as you sit stunned at the mere accumulation
of words filed, edited, viewed, inserted,
formatted, spun into websites, downloaded
and upgraded into numbers nothing but infinity
seems able to record, even now
on some desk, maybe yours, in an old jelly jar,
or a ceramic elephant with a hole in its back
that your niece in third grade gave you for Christmas,

6

or in a German beer stein or handpainted wooden
Chinese calligrapher's pen holder, sprouts a fistful
of pencils, Roethke's preservers of dolor, each one waiting
as it always has, to lie like a faithful love
between your thumb and finger, to let your words
be the only ones they will ever know
even as they give themselves to the alchemy
of everything, becoming empty phrases,
an X to mark the spot, reminders
to pick up bread and coffee, maybe a note
written to a friend whose dog has died.

This Is Another Reason to Write a Poem

When Frank Sinatra died, my mother called,
said, "Well, that's it," and hung up. She'd
been one of the sweet-toothed bobbysoxers
standing in line for hours, looking
in the windows at the diamonds, dresses, shoes
they'd never have. Step by saddle-shoed step, she
moved toward the stage, smoothing down her skirt;
tugging her sunlight-white blouse, cut close
at her waist, open through the first three buttons;
feeling her way to a wink, that grin, the song.
"When he was young, your father looked
like Sinatra," she told me once after laughing
at "What's a seven-letter word for ol' blue eyes?"
"He was cute like Frank. And tough, too." Later,
she took my sister and me to see the Beatles.
The girl next to us broke her seat jumping on it.
My mother tapped her on the shoulder and
yelled, "Don't ever forget." In 1984 she
went to see Bruce Springsteen, and within a month
had all the videos, recordings, black sweatshirts,
hung his photo in the family room. She wears
a tour T-shirt to bed. Each morning, before she
fixes her toast, she plays "Born in the USA,"
"Tunnel of Love," or "She's the One." Tonight
I called her. I had a joke. She told me about her line-
dance lessons and how she walks around the lake
with the economics prof. "He's good company.
Doesn't have much." She told me the boy had been there

to mow, and the grass is brown and that the Fourth of July
will be fun because a big band will be playing "In the
    Mood"
and "Star Dust" before the fireworks. I told her
our gardens are blooming, and she told me the straw-
    berries
were good this year and that she'd invited six people
for dinner next week and thinks she'll make the meal
now and freeze it. It went on like this and then she said,
"That's enough chitchat, love ya, honey," and hung up,
and I knew she'd take a bath, stay up to watch the news,
    then
walk to bed in her T-shirt with the crossword and a cup of
    tea.

Against Elegies

I'm tired of Death's allure,
of how the old beggar
makes me think that
rowing across the river is
somehow richer, more serious, than
the center of a pomegranate or my
dog's way of sleeping on his paws.
I'm tired of "the beauty of the elegy,"
the tone-deaf lyricism of it all. I
want Death to listen for a while
to Bud Powell or Art Blakey,
to have to stare for seven hours
at Matisse. I want him to do
stand-up and play the banjo, to
have to tap dance and juggle, to
play Trivial Pursuit and weed
my garden. I'm tired of how Death
throws his voice, gets us
to judge a begonia, a song
in the shower, a voice, an old dog.
I want life's ragged way
of getting along, the wasted
afternoon and empty morning, the
sloppy kiss. I want to stagger
along between innings. I want
the burnt toast, the forgotten note,
the lost pillowcase, the dime
novel, the Silly Putty of it all.

Rainbow

"There is no precise date at which mythology gave way to science."
—Carl B. Boyer, *The Rainbow: From Myth to Mathematics*

So science is the bully on the playground,
the guy who says Babe Ruth was just
a drunk, the kid who rolls his eyes
the day the trees all bud. You know elves
live under your porch, that God loves
puppets, that the wind comes from a witch's
cave, and birds sing just to sing. What if
Wordsworth, strolling along the lakes,
had looked up, taken out his pen, and speculated
how the color came from light refracted
through the drops of rain that formed
around some dust? And what if Noah, crazed
with the smell of dung, the impatience of every
creature on the earth, what if this wild builder
of faith, when he saw that covenant of color
draping over his mad zoo, had tried to tabulate
the cubits in the rainbow's length, forgetting
about the dove, the olive branch, dry land?
And what do we make of Philip, Plato's less-
than-certain pal? He scribbled in his notebook
that the rainbow wasn't stable after all; it moved
as the observer moved and somewhere
over the rainbow was farther away
than any bluebird could ever fly.
So if science is as uncertain
as tomorrow's weather, I think I'll say

the rainbow, like most everything—this
poem, elephants, the hurricane along
the Georgia coast, my daughter's scribbled
chalk across the sidewalk—is not just one more
worn, anonymous effect in cause's long and
flagrant history. I'll say the rainbow simply
comes. Light may bend, reflect, refract,
but why then color? Why Mozart
from a catgut string? And why this morning,
when I saw that we were out of coffee,
did I look up and see you in the garden,
staking our tomatoes in the rain?

Framing the Morning

Next to the sofa, books: an atlas, the poems of John Clare,
    a guide to wildflowers.

The sudden lash of light across the kitchen windowsill—
    the silver top of the pepper mill
    the pale yellow of the egg timer
    the sparkle of whisks.

Under the hemlock, empty seed cases across the mulch,
    dark droppings left by the scatter of sparrows.

In the branches, chickadees, nuthatches, cardinals, then
    the flash of a goldfinch;
    across the yard, the cat curled by a rotting stump.

Clouds come. The sun lifts itself into the crown of trees.
    The leaves quiver.

Toast. Currant jam. Coffee with cream. The chipped
    plate with the half-moon painted in its center.

Out by the swatch of jewelweed and daylilies, two chairs.
    The light falls across them,
    their shadows growing longer.

The morning paper, folded open to the crossword.

On the porch, a blanket and binoculars.

After Reading Dom John Chapman,
Benedictine Abbot

"Pray as you can; not as you can't."

My prayers will sit on the backs
of bedraggled donkeys, in the sidecars
of Harleys, in the pockets of night
watchmen, on the laps of widows.
They will be the stones I walk by,
the smudges I leave on anything I touch,
the last place the last snow melts. They
will be brown, weekdays, potato pancakes.
They will stick to the undersides of porches,
docks, dog paws, and carpets. When I'm sick,
my cough will carry them. When you leave
in the morning, they will sink into the bed,
the sofa, every towel. I will carry them
in the modesty of my feet. Everything
will be praying. My dog will be petitioning
for mercy when he stops to sniff a post.
Every window in our house will be
an offering for supplication. The birds
at the feeder will be twitching
for my sins. I will say my prayers
are bread dough, doorknobs, golf tees,
any small and nameless change of heart.
When I forget my prayers, they will
bundle up and go out on their own
across the street, down into the basement,
into a small town with no mayor where

there is a single swing in the park. When
I forget, they'll know I was watching TV,
the sky, or listening to Basie, remembering
the way my mother and father jitterbugged
to the big band station, he pulling her close,
then spinning her out across the green kitchen floor.

Learning from Old Houses

"The house talks, as old houses do."
—Gladys Taber, *Stillmeadow Sampler*

Our house tells us not to worry
about the weeds in the yard. It says,
"Rain, driveway, corner cupboard," says,
"backdoor, hinge about to give in to rust."
And we listen, against a cracked window, along
the paint-chipped banister leading to the basement,
back among the canned tomatoes, in the corner
with the week's laundry. We walk through, nudging
a book back into place, straightening a family photo.
Dust now stays put along the edges of the stairs,
shelves, dinner plates, in any corner of any wall,
picture frame, mirror, in every crack
of each ceramic elephant, angel, flowerpot. We
keep a vase of fresh flowers on the kitchen table,
change the water once, then pick a fistful of new
blooms or in the winter bring some home with
the cereal, coffee, prescriptions. The house
tells us to go to bed early, reminds us
our children are gone and we need to keep
the thermostat at 70. It advises us about the mail,
the storm coming in a couple of minutes,
and that the neighbors are changing their curtains,
putting up their screens, mowing their lawns,
leaving. It quietly lets us know about the draft
under the backdoor, the mildew on the porch,
the paint peeling in the entryway. We have

nothing to say. We stay. We get up
before the sun comes in the windows,
and we listen for our own slow quiet finding its place.

Last Chores of Fall

The trace of October lingering
along the ridge behind our house,
the exhale of yellow-gold
within the stagger of oaks
tells us it is time to move inside,
let our blood return to its quiet
wander, the year now browning
toward a sudden frost. This
afternoon I will slowly uproot
the impatiens, tossing
their gasps of pink, white,
and salmon into the dark
of the compost pile. Remembering
to bend at the knees, I'll carry
the cracked and chipped pots
back to the garden's shed,
stack them, letting the clay
of one pot settle into the dirt
in another. I'll bring in
the geraniums, their twisted,
leggy stems nearly leafless,
and cut them down to hopeful
nubs, then set them on the sill.
The dogs will watch as I wash
and dry the trowel my father
used for thirty years. Each
year he added another row
or two of flowers. I'll hang

the trowel on its rusty nail.
The dogs will lift their mysterious
noses into the changing air, into
the smells of mud, moldering
leaves, the scent of approaching
snow along the stream below
the barren ridge. Then I will
turn back to the house, the sun
burning down early into its setting.

Fractals

On this autumn afternoon, the light
falls across the last sentence in a letter,
just before the last movement of Brahms's
Fourth Symphony, a recording made more
than twenty years ago, the time when we were
looking for a house to rehabilitate, maybe
take out a wall and let the kitchen open
up into the living room, put in a window
so the morning light could fall across
the bed my wife's grandmother made
the canopy for, the bed she slept in for
forty years. She was a doctor looking
for a town close enough that we can
drive past where she practiced, imagine
her picking up her violin when there
was time between patients, settle
it under her chin and play, looking
out the window onto the same street we
drive down on our way to visit our
daughter in her studio. She creates
dresses, stitches turning into lines,
fabric turning into sculpture hanging
under her skylight, the dresses' threads
knotted, their edges frayed.
When we knock on her door, she
welcomes us with cups of steaming
tea, turns down the jazz and kisses us.
She is happy in this light, and later she

will ask us how we like our new place,
laugh when we begin to tell her all
our plans for tearing out the kitchen,
knocking out a wall so we can see
deep into the wood, along the creek
that twists itself around a pile of rocks
and through the trees. She makes us
dinner as we listen to Miles Davis,
"Birth of the Cool"—I always wonder
why he ended with a vocal, one
that sounds recorded twenty years
before. Its notes are sleepy,
the voices like smoke. At home
the dog and cats are sleeping. We
forgot to leave a light on for them,
but the radio is playing, and when we
get there, they will want to go outside.
The dog will pause for a scratch behind
his ears, his tail wagging as the cats
jump off the couch, hurry out the door,
disappear into the dark.
We'll tune the radio to a symphony,
watch the moon harvesting
its light through the back window.

Fragments from the Early Morning

This then will be the end, a stone
left here under the comfrey

Sores on the brook trout, quiet
coming under the weak knees of the gardener

In the valley, the crown vetch, traveler's
sidecar, no one else

One oriole, its bubble of song, orange
on the leaves

The wind,
the saw blade
still whining in the wood

The cat, back in, asleep on the chair

Winter lowering its arms, the homeless
playing jacks under the bridge

Cars in the parking lots,
dishes stacked in the kitchen

The fallen log

The Last Thing

That's Jesus with the head of a tuna
sailing on his cross, over the roofs,
over villagers going to market, fixing
their cars, making soup, taking
their medicine or watching each other

on TV. See how the clouds hang
there around him? He loves that. He
even tosses dice inside them to make
it rain. Sometimes he just lies back,
like here in this one, and lets everything

alone. He knows so long as he's here
on this cross, everyone will let him be.
He loves how they had him rise
and come for dinner. See, here in
this one how he's having some chocolate

cake? Outside, leaning against the front
of the house is his cross. See the dog
licking its paw? And the half-moon with
Jesus sitting on it? Last night
I started a new painting. I

really like all the cows in this one.
I like that green sky and that little
girl pulling the wagon of doll's heads.
And I like the old guy sitting on that
fish. That was the last thing I put in.

This Was My Real Life

I was born in the backseat of a trolley
going to the ballpark on opening day.

Two policemen once gave me a ticket
to the circus. I was playing in the street,
rolling a ball over the crosswalk.

In math class I tried to have the train
that was leaving Seattle at 10 A.M.
on its way to Dallas jump the tracks
after it crossed the bridge outside Omaha.

Wolves raised me. We played a game
with sticks and moss. They left when I was twelve.

I never married. I built
two houses, one where my father
had his woodworking shop, one where
my mother shot our dog.

In the winter, after a heavy snowfall,
I would listen to Verdi and read
want ads looking for things people
needed that I didn't want to sell.

I was a failure at board games.
I was a failure at knowing
the names of flowers. I
was a failure at knowing when to leave.

When I was twenty-seven, I left home
for Mexico, stopped in Oklahoma,
went instead to the Florida Keys,
stayed forty-two years in a house a friend
had owned before he died
in a diving accident.
I ate fish and painted houses.

One summer, I didn't paint, quit
for the season, bought a pickup,
slept in its bed, drove on and off
to my mother's grave, sat there
reading self-help books. On the way
home, I always stopped at Parrot Jungle.

Waiting with William Stafford in an Oregon Airport

This morning, the rain on the tarmac
is the same gray as the sky. You
aren't here of course, gone
years ago. I wonder
how many times you waited
in your own quiet for a flight,
raising your eyebrows, lowering
them just as fast. You would have
glanced at the toddler, watched
how the child hides under the seat,
giggles toward her tired mother
trying even in this hour to be good.
A dozen travelers look out
into the mountains, each
lost—in an old conversation,
a hidden sorrow, some tiny
hope. It's December 11, the date
my mother's father died in 1943.
Christmas carols lighten the air,
a dulcimer bringing us "Greensleeves,"
"It Came upon a Midnight Clear,"
"Do You Hear What I Hear?"
The evening my grandfather died,
his lungs swollen with tuberculosis,
my mother and grandmother
heard him singing "May Time."
My mother was pregnant with me.
She still sings that song.

Each year she buys tulips.
My father was in Belgium.
For two years the women grieved
and listened to the news. Soon
after my father came home,
TB was over like the war.
It's time to board. The passengers
walk toward the gate. I
have an hour before my flight.
When you looked out through
the barbed wire of the camp
did you feel your poems waiting to go home?

Toys in the Attic

"As you collect more and more information, your mental
attic never fills, but it certainly gets cluttered."
—David G. Myers, *Psychology*

Even if you need those green slippers,
that teapot with the broken handle, or
Cousin Benny's wire rims, you will
never find them. And if you want to
reread the letters from the lover you met
in Amsterdam, find your appointment book
from your first job, or look over the scorecards
from the times you cheated at golf or bridge,
they're there, but you won't know where.
You can look under your uncle's army uniform,
behind the cracked mirror, among the hundreds
of *Time* magazines, even sort through that tangle
of earrings, belts, ties, bracelets, scarves, and
frayed extension cords, but nothing will
turn up. Everything's a kitten slipping under
the wicker chair. What was the name
of the shop that closed last summer?
Was it chocolate she was allergic to? Why
did they both hate the eighteenth century?
A chickadee remembers every one
of the four hundred spots it's hidden seed.
You would flutter into starvation. So,
your freezer has a dozen six-packs
of English muffins, seven half-gallons
of strawberry ice cream, and enough

chicken potpies to feed a summer camp.
You have car keys in every room, lists
that say things like "send birthday card
to Tom; he's 72," and a notebook filled
with reminders such as "Don't tell the joke
about the chicken and the welder anymore."
Then sometimes, usually after you've
weeded the flower bed, or read a chapter
in the novel for the book club you think
meets a week from today, you sit down,
maybe with a cup of strong coffee, maybe
with some wine or a beer and see yourself
up in that attic, finding your puppets, your skates,
and the maps you stared at for hours.

St. Francis in Disney World

The children come up to him, touch
his robe and giggle. He blesses them. They
run to ask their parents to take their photo
peeking out from behind his filthy holiness.
Mickey quietly comes up beside him, his
huge fingers dangling like loaves of Wonder
Bread, tilts his head as if to say, You better
leave, take a bath, put on clean jeans.
St. Francis whispers, asking for the birds.
Mickey shakes his head. St. Francis holds
his place in line, each ride spinning its
squealing riders round or up or down: a
chug, a plunge, a long and hopeless cast
of thousands, tons of hot dogs, fries, and
pizza, sushi, Coke and Pepsi, pie and
ice cream, chocolate. There are bees.
He has no ticket. He's told to step aside.
He looks up where the sky should be. He
watches a cat slide under a plastic
elephant. He looks back up. The sky
has gone. The earth has gone. His feet
are sore. His hands are turning into
birds. His hood is filling up with coins.
His beard is filled with bells.

The Crank Collector

I'd love to rust.
Just sit there
turning into air.
Now, I put cranks
on anything. See
how I put one
on that lawn deer.
I wasn't sure where
to fasten it. When I
found this old stuffed
chair I had to put
a crank on it. I
thought this stump
should have one.
And that one
on the rowboat, I first
put on our bed. I find
cranks everywhere.
They just turn up,
in the woods for instance,
behind a garage. I found
one once in a cemetery.
The one on the side of
the house I found while
digging in my garden,
planting some spurge.
There are a couple
thousand kinds of spurge.

That crank there's
a double handle. You
can swing it arm over
arm. This one I painted
green before I stuck it
into that window box.
And I took that one from
my grandmother's attic.
I thought she'd like it
fastened to her Bible.

That's Enough

At times like these, we should
sit down, maybe pet our dogs,
or listen to the way even Bach
left out notes. We should have
a sandwich, something light,
thick tomato slices, lettuce,
slather on the mayonnaise.
I wonder how fish let their
impulses settle in their cells.
Sit down. Just sit, there,
on that end of the couch. Let
your arm drape over the side.
Imagine the wind has come
through the window, has turned
itself into a garden monk who is
opening his sack, flicking his
bamboo fan in front of your face.
Let every word in the world
become a vireo. Let them
overrun the yard. We'll count
back into yesterday, the widower
knocking at the back door.

The Mail Carrier

When the weather is good,
she imagines each letter
sits forever in a lonely
mind. Postcards, a small
hello, sometimes a question
about the job help her
believe the uniform,
the truck, even the sack
keep her safe from
her own days. She often
daydreams she's an angel
carrying the mystery
of words that only connect.
She thinks about her route,
how she's driven it
for twenty-seven years: five miles
north, two more east,
four south, six west,
tires over the same roads,
her hand reaching across
the empty passenger seat,
settling it all into
each mailbox, a quiet pause
in front of every house.
She knows by now what lies
in nearly every envelope,
and knows when she gives up

this work, she'll dream
the route, carry opened,
unread letters throughout the day.

Tinnitus

I live between the tines of a tuning fork,
caught without a partner in the middle
of a one-note waltz. Philip Glass is Bach.

A hummingbird whirs among blossoms
savoring the sweet nectar it has no choice
but to gather. A chickadee pauses or waits

for a mate after singing its singular song.
The crow's harsh caw or the owl's haunting
E minor arrives with some surprise, even

delight. But this terminally shrill pitch lies
taut as a high wire stretched between
Ravel's "Bolero" and "Harold in Italy,"

between the wind through the winter's
trees and the burble of a woodland stream,
between you on my left and you on my right.

"Good night." "Good morning." "I love you."
"I no longer love you," each a sentry, and I
am in the center hearing and listening and

following the steadfast cadence of this whistle
without a train. This is not a "ringing in the ears."
That can lead to melody or counterpoint, a benign

accompaniment to the day's cacophony.
A ringing could bring you someone
stopping by, a wrong number, the echo

of a wedding or a funeral, the end of round seven.
But in this high-pitched world there is no variation
on the theme, no largo, obbligato, pizzicato, rest.

It is Mozart, old, alone, remembering one tone, one note.

Out in the Fields with the Dogs
a Week before Christmas

Their great white heads take me
deeper into the snow. They
lift their noses into the air, then
push further into the drifts,
finding the lost smells held
to the roots, the weeds, and
matted ground cover. They know
the deer have walked here, their
own heads lifted high into the
morning. I can only imagine
what worlds fill the dogs' heads,
what takes form from the thousand
smells we can never know, their
dreams made from all these grasses,
mud, scat, and fur. Maybe something
takes the scents and stirs them into
some bewilderment of wolves
walking a ridge. We walk on.
At home, the Christmas tree is
trimmed with strings of tiny lights,
glitter-covered glass, tinsel, angels,
nesting birds, toy drums, and
the withering paper globes we
made when we were children.
You are baking *kolačes.* You are
baking them the way my father did,
rolling the soft dough over the

apricots, raisins, apples, and poppy seed.
The snow is falling harder. The dogs
look back, then run to my side, sit
and gnaw at the ice frozen to their feet.
This year it will be the two of us
and the dogs. We've been told
the full moon is to be the brightest
it's been in 133 years. We'll watch
it through the bedroom window as
it crosses through the trees, low
in the southern sky, the dogs
asleep at the foot of the bed.

The Materialism of Angels

"Who would say that pleasure is not useful?"
—Charles Eames

Of course the angels dance. If not
on the head of a pin, then along
any boardwalk beside the ocean of stars.
And they eat hot and spicy: salsa,
Tabasco, red peppers. They love
mangoes. They can munch
for hours on cashews. Olives
sit in bronze bowls on the cherry
tables next to their canopy beds
where the solace of pillows swallows
their sweet heads and the quiet
of silk lies across their happy backs.
They know the altruism of material things.
They want to say to us, "We'll sleep
next to you. Feel our soft and unimposing
flutter across your shoulders, on your
heartbroken feet." They want us
to take, eat, smell the wood,
run our tired fingers over the rim of
every glass, give our eyes the chance
to see the metal bend and
curve its way into the black oval
of the chair. They want us to feel
the holiness of scratching where it
itches, rubbing where it hurts. They
want us to take long, steamy showers

and a nap. They know how easily
we follow directions: hook the red wire
to the front of the furnace, fill in only
the top half of the life insurance form.
They have no manuals for joy.
They can't fix anything we break.
They wonder why we never laugh
enough, why we don't know God
is crazy for deep massage and loves
to wail an alto sax whenever they dance.

II
Quantum Theory

I Am Wearing Your Shirt

For my father

When your words left
your hands, the only place
silence holds us to the earth
opened. Somewhere a child
opened a door. Somewhere
a mother looked out a window.

You lived in your hands—alive
in bread dough, along the handles
of tools, holding the endless
usefulness of rags. "In all
things, a firm grip," you told me,
and at the end, you wanted only
your hands.

The snow that comes in the mornings
brings each of your words. The water
forms around your *and,* your *either, not,*
and *yes.* They land, they just land.
Sometimes they fall all day, and into
the next. Sometimes they melt before noon.

You never waited. In the spring
you forced the shoots, even
the blooms. The trays waited
on the coffee table, the refrigerator,
the floor of the family room. We gave

one to anyone who stopped. They
were gone by May.

Yesterday, I found a photograph. I'm
sitting on your shoulders. Or is it you
sitting on your father's shoulders? Or
is it your grandfather sitting
on his beer wagon, holding
his team of tired horses?

At the funeral, you walked through the house
collecting your garden tools, cookbooks, and
sweatshirts while each visitor laid the bud
of a rose on your chest. They formed a heart
within the heart of your arms and folded hands.
I imagine them opening in your ashes.

Every morning for fifty-one years, you
woke and began by whispering, "This
is the best part of the day," and laid
your arm across her back.

I am wearing your shirt. Now,

when I walk, I wear your hat. In
the garden, I wear your gloves.

Here the land is flat. You
lived in the clay hills,
always at an angle.

Growing up on Goat Shit Hill,
looking out over the sullen
open hearths, the tired smoke
of the mills, the smudged strip
of heartless coal, you took shot
after shot at the hoop your father
rammed into the ridge behind
your house, knowing any miss
could send you down a mile
after the disrespected ball.

The house is cold now, cold
as spring turning itself
into bloom. We wait at the window.

Your God wanted no attention at all.

Yesterday, when I dug into our garden's
matted earth, I felt your hand slide
into mine as if it were putting on
a glove. We went together
into the awkward ground, turned the soil,
let it slip between our fingers.

You always stepped aside
to let every question have its way.

Where have you walked
in a year? The center
of snow . . . the center of

each amen . . . of every
word we've tried to keep.
Now, on this still April afternoon,
a year to the day you came
to stay within us, the trees'
negative space waits for leaves.

Wearing your shirt, I look out into
the wood, where the end of each branch
touches the air's one silence.

How you loved this dust, this
light on the side of the house.

Worn Morning

For Heather McHugh

How to say this in the words that now
are tired even of themselves

Water-on-the-garden
Sure foot along the river
Long note of the full moon

We listen, one hand resting on another

Yesterday, as the blanket of anger
covered us, the earth did its single task

Our sleep keeps coming back

Then—

Into the day

Into the day

Once after a full night of rain, after
the lightning and thunder, we walked out
looking at the glisten of the sky's sure language

But today, how to find the last noun
and its only verb

Wind chime
Dust
Driftwood keeping to itself

Last night, my wife placed a handful of rose petals
in a cup on the woodstove
Now sleep takes her where she can be herself

Soft pulse of the sprinkler on the garden

Soon the children down the street
will be in their yard,
their voices saying why

The words travel along with their unhappy endings

The honeysuckle is a weaving of bees

When I Was Conceived

The war would go on for two more years
and that was the same time a Pentecostal
uprising took over our unlocked village.
Everyone was speaking in tongues.
At Gilliland's Grocery checkout line, suddenly
cornflakes, a head of lettuce, a pound of ground
round would set off a chaos of glossolalia.
I heard later that in a town about ten miles
from ours eleven toymakers had gotten
together and things turned dark: they
began cutting off the hind legs of hobby
horses, the left hands of marionettes.
"It was a strange and unsettling time,"
my grandmother would whisper whenever
I asked her to tell the story. "I would try
to read," she'd say, her eyes darting
from one corner of the room to another,
"but the words kept skipping to the next
page. It was useless. I baked and waited
for you to be born and for your father
to come home. My tongue felt tired all
the time." When spring came, the daffodils
opened and the crocuses survived the last
frost and the tangle of gray branches
began to quiver with green. "I suppose
your sister will grow up to make circus tents
out of her old dresses," my grandmother
would often say to my mother. "But I've never

had a sister," my mother would tell her again.
"I've never had a sister" is what she says
now when I visit her. "Who are you?"
I never spoke in tongues.
By the time I was in junior high school,
the evangelist wore out, began to seduce
the widowed sisters who lived on the corner
across from the park, ended up saying
not much more than "I'd like a double scoop
of orange pineapple" at the ice cream shop
near the edge of town. I wandered into growing up,
getting my hair cut, listening to my grandmother,
tithing 10 percent of my allowance, and getting
mostly A's in math and B's in everything else.

What Then

Not now was what my mother said, always
said, every day said like a bagel left on the shelf
or seven boxes of paper clips. I remember
it was a late afternoon after school, after
the lethargic bus filled with sweat and hair
and those spiral notebooks that had a Panther
on the cover had hauled the day's time back
to snacks: Zebra Cakes, cheese twirls, jelly
donuts, Coke, milk, Ding Dongs. It was
on one of those rides *not now* took over
and my hands went deep into my pockets,
and I knew there was no place God
could be alone and no place I could go
and no place I could play catch
or bake a fish sandwich or lay cement.
The stars were as close
as they would ever get,
and the leaves on every tree had no idea
they were on a tree like the way the moon
kept changing through each month
even when it rose over Ted's Garage,
like a bicycle left out under a bridge.
So, I sat out on the back porch
and imagined I was on the back porch
and half-expected the house to stay
where it was while my mother tucked
the sheets around my pillow and smoothed
the covers after I made the bed. I knew

I'd turned out the light, but after that,
the small bones in my wrist seemed
like words that had no idea what sentence
they were in, and my eyes just looked out
over the long slow green of the backyard.

Forgetting How to Sleep

Every Sunday my father would open the back door
and say the church was a dent in his car.
He kept the family Chevy clean.
My sister and I would watch out
the windows, two birds, two questions,
as we drove to his mother's hydrangea-
smothered trailer, sitting alone
on the stained outskirts of Pittsburgh.
She lived with her salt and pepper shakers
and the August heat and her husband. She
was a fur coat, a couple of Manhattans, and
an ashtray, lavender, bee stings. She laughed
in spite of her eyes. We'd watch the staggering
clouds and pull down the skin under our eyes
and stretch our lips wide across our faces.
The church was silly, lopsided, and bald.
It was a cracked window. I suppose
we suffered. My father said we ate.
He told us how his mother
carried an old hoe and walked around the lawn
looking for snow peas. Later, she'd give him a nickel
and tell him snow peas turned your blood sunny.
We'd drive through the town where my father
was a kid. "There's where I bowled," he'd say.
"There's where they found Mrs. Simpson."
We'd watch the broken windows, see
the bent stop sign, and the hummingbird
feeder outside Frampton's Hardware Store.

My father would say, "I see something
that is tangerine." At my grandmother's,
we'd sit and watch her husband try to talk.
Once when we got there around three
in the afternoon, he was sitting in front
of the refrigerator, on a ladder, asleep,
his head in the freezer. It was always
August and always the weekend. It
was always sometime after church.

The Remote

I'm on the couch, rambling
around with the remote, channels
flashing in from 2 to 734. I can send
a wrestler hurtling into a low-
pressure system over Tennessee.
A televangelist preaching in a French
provincial bedroom can be readying
to sleep with Vanna White who has
added a vowel to Emeril's "bam"
of oregano before he survives
a NASCAR crash. But Andy and Opie
come walking through the woods
without a single thought of a DVD,
cell phone, download, or this remote.

In 1949 my grandmother bought
the first television in her town,
a chunky Dumont. I can still see
me, six years old, coming into
her living room, hearing
what I thought was the radio,
although my grandmother never
listened to the radio after my
grandfather died singing along
to the song they'd called their own.
When I came around the corner,
there was the TV flickering
on its impossible screen,

the Cisco Kid and Pancho
laughing in the living room.

The shows were scattered through
her day, and she and I would sit together
on the couch, play along to a morning
game show, watch Kay Newman cook
in her Pittsburgh kitchen, one light
hanging over her bobbed hair, then
catch the noon news. Mid-afternoon
the curtains would open on Kukla,
Fran, and Ollie and we'd sing
"Here we are again! Here we are
again," and then we'd crown the
Queen for a Day. At dinner, we
set trays between us and the TV
while around an old upright,
Buzz 'n' Bill crooned, "A cup
of coffee, a sandwich, and you."

Each evening, Captain Video
and the Video Ranger flashed through
space, and even on the night half
their cardboard ship collapsed
Captain kept his cool and let the set
lean on his shoulder while he steered
us out of range of the Martian's deadly
ray, never dreaming that in twenty years
a kid watching him now would dream
of hopping on the surface of the moon.

My grandmother and I sat amazed.
If a station blinked off, I'd get up,
walk to the set, and twist the dial.
We'd watch almost anything.
But I can still hear her voice
sounding the way it did when
a tiresome neighbor left
after "just popping in."
"Skip the hearings, Honey.
That man bores me. Hand me
my Johnny Walker Red.
Let's watch another game show."

The Ace of Spades

My grandmother said I should
know about the bullet. When I
asked her why, she said, "You
need to." Today, shuffling
the cards for a game with
my mother, I stopped at
the ace of spades, turned it
over, put it back into the deck
thinking about the time my father
drove for twenty-one hours to get home
for a weekend. It was January.
The snow was blizzard thick,
and the temperature had dropped
to the teens. I had gone to bed
warm. When I asked where
he'd been, my mother said,
"Europe. I've told you that."
Falling asleep, I could see
only a long day of sleet, my
father's boots caked with mud,
the huge tires of his truck spinning
into another lost town. My mother
lives with us now, and I remember
how every day my grandmother
played game after game of solitaire.
Each time, she'd work through
the deck just once. "That's
the real way to play," she'd say.

Sorting through the Records

"I need to toss the ones I'll never
listen to," my mother writes, "or I
could give them to Grace who'd
sell them at the Lutheran Home."
I can see my mother dusting off
each record, setting aside those
she doesn't remember, coming
across the ones that take her
back to the dance floor where
she jitterbugged, fox-trotted,
and slow danced with my father.
"I can still see your father and me,
dancing to 'Polka Dots and
Moonbeams.' My dress
had polka dots. That's dumb, I know."
It was 1940. The war was waiting
for my father. He graduated on Sunday,
the next day took a bus to boot camp,
became a black company's captain
and slogged through the mud of France
and Belgium, then into the jungle rot
of the Philippines. Through basic
he ate, slept, bathed with the white
soldiers, used the whites-only toilets,
drank from the fountains just for whites.
At the day's end, he saluted his men,
then dismissed them to their sergeant.
"I thought that's just the way it was,"

he said only once, his brow furrowed
like the rows the tanks cut deep
in the camp dust. Every week, he
wrote my mother ending always
with the same PS: "I know this war
will never end." She waited.
One New Year's Eve he sent her
violets from France. She pinned them
on her coat, stood outside, listened
to the clang and clamor of midnight.
Tonight she'll put on Frank Sinatra
singing "I Bought You Violets for
Your Furs." Later in the week she'll
go out line dancing with some friends.

February Is No Month to Move

My mother wants to stay
by the phone, wants to sift
through all the letters.
The ice has built up
on the roof, hangs
in dripping exclamation
marks along the gutters.
She wants to know about
the end tables, wonders
if anyone will want the desk.
She has twenty-three creamers.
Along the hallway hang
the photographs of her father,
his mother, cousins, grandchildren,
my father in his Army uniform,
my sister and her family. She
looks out the window. The sky
is the color of the clay
my father worked to grow
his vegetables and flowers.
She asks me about the daybed
on the porch. I put the garden tools
in my car, come back in.
She's looking at my father's shoes.
She asks me about her newspaper.

During the Last Two Weeks of His Life,
He Wrote Only the Last Lines of Poems

I

the stars, lost in the half-light of evening.

II

giving us only a noun and the time to understand it.

III

after the taxi, after the end of the affair.

IV

like the slow ruin of his own small town.

V

and God? Lost somewhere in the bread section.

VI

wind, three medieval priests, a puppet, and a wedding
    dress.

VII

the bus.

VIII

window, pouring out the last of the anonymous gin.

IX

not the cow, not the fence post, not even the back door.

X

knew the rest, but kept the pile beside her desk, adding to
it when it snowed.

XI

amid the holiness of snails.

XII

later. Then he juggled a scarf, an orange ball, and his
flute.

XIII

was it the rain, was it the ontology of morning?

Waking Up in a Cold Sweat

The first thing you do is feel under the bed
just to make sure that the hag with the yellow towel
who was rubbing it over your feet while she smiled
off into the stars isn't lying there waiting to grab
your ankle when you make your first step
into the unknown of the day. Then you lie
back down and wonder what it means
that you were being chased by turtles
the size of Ohio while a flock of magpies,
the tips of their ragged wings touching your hair,
floated back and forth overhead, shrieking something
that sounded like what your third-grade teacher said
when she handed back your arithmetic,
the fractured sums scarred by her bloody pencil.
And what about the big, fire engine–red wax lips
your grandmother held up on her dinner fork?
It's all too much, too much for
even Breton to wage a manifesto
against business suits or the rise
of poststructural analyses of French
cuisine. You think maybe you were raised
by wolves after all, one dressed as an accountant
with a twitch in his left eyebrow, the other
a packaging designer who won't let you wrap
the stuffed donkey you got for your best friend.
You remember the time at recess when
the thug who slouched in the last seat
of your row stared up at you from the bottom

of the slide. You wonder if you had written
your aunt a thank-you note, or shoveled
the snow from the front steps like you said
you would, if you had gone deaf during
the children's sermon about the lies
we don't even know we tell. Then you remember
the fourth glass of wine, the extra cup of coffee,
the late movie on the horror channel, the anchovies,
your daughter's date from the night before,
your son's arm in a cast, the project deadline
you missed by a week, the bruise on your shin
you've noticed every day for a over a month,
and you know everything's fine. On the other side
of the bed, you hear the long breathing of your marriage,
and you fluff up your pillow, let
your arm lie across the space between you,
let your quieting fingers wait for the alarm.

Hands

My grandfather grew up holding rags,
pounding his fist into the pocket
of a ball glove, gripping a plumb line
for his father who built what anyone
needed. At sixteen, wanting to work on
his own, he lied about his age
and for forty-nine years carried his lunch
to the assembly line where he stood
tightening bolts on air brake after
air brake along the monotonous belt.
I once asked him how he did that all
those years. He looked at me, said,
"I don't understand. It was only
eight hours a day," then closed
his fists. Every night after dinner
and a pilsner, he worked some more.
In the summer, he'd turn the clay,
grow tomatoes, turnips, peas,
and potatoes behind borders
of bluebells and English daisies,
and marigolds to keep away the rabbits.
When the weather turned to frost,
he went to the basement where,
until the seeds came in March,
he made perfect picture frames, each
glistening with layers of sweet shellac.
His hands were never bored. Even
in his last years, arthritis locking every

knuckle, he sat in the kitchen carving
wooden houses you could set on a shelf,
one after another, each one different.

Tabula Rasa

"You may lose the ability to use your right hand."
—Surgeon's diagnosis

I think about the end of writing and what may follow:
Some sunlight across the bowl on the kitchen table.

A daughter stopping by after work. I'll lift the cup
of coffee with my left hand. We will laugh.

The dogs will wrestle, the older one letting
the pup pull tufts of hair from his scraggly ears.

The geese will still bring their V, north then south.
I know a solitary one will fly by and I will wonder

about its being alone, if it will find its way.
I won't know. You'll say,

"Go ahead, stir the soup, add some more
tomatoes if you like, or maybe some oregano."

I will use the phone, but I'm used to stamps,
love writing a name and address, their steady

place floating in the center of a moving
universe, then adding where to return

the letter if it doesn't find its way and needs
to wander back. Up there, in the left corner.

That's a kind of home. And in the center, another.
And there we are, heading out, hoping we connect

without knowing when. Maybe not even where.

The Salt and Pepper Collector

She works at night, never
saying a word, assembling
salt and pepper shakers
around the edges of her
house: the foundation, on
windowsills, up walls, up
the posts holding up
the porch, along the roof,
along the stone walk leading
to the red front door, along
the walk as it winds around
the side to the stoop and up
to the yellow door. Flamingoes
stand with potbellied burghers,
elephants, watering cans, cats
and dogs, windmills, angels,
hats, houses, locomotives,
frogs, and eggs. As a child,
she talked to birds, told
the grackles, chickadees,
and jays that she knew how
to fly. She buried her mother
under a summer's moon while
in the meadow behind the house,
deer watched her, their quiet
faces still above the grasses.
People drop off shakers all
the time. She watches them

out the window. They wave
and leave. She sleeps all
afternoon. At night, she
watches the moon move
through the stars, tries to
see God shake some salt and
pepper down across her house.

The Sculptor of TV

Pointing at the pile
of televisions rising
up in his garage, he
points at a console
balancing on a tiny
set and on it three
with ten-inch screens
and on those, two
twenty-inchers, then
on top of it, a twelve-
inch one. On top of it
all, a cabinet, and set
inside, a tiny circus:
four clowns, three
elephants, a troupe
of acrobats, and high
above them all,
a tightrope walker, crossing
over, holding an umbrella.
He plugs in the bottom
set, extends his arm,
smiles, and each screen
comes to light with news
and weather, baseball
games, evangelists.
When he changes
a channel the tightrope
walker flips, hanging
from the wire by his knees.

The Time between Mornings

Sometimes it's late and you
can't sleep. The sun has gone
shining somewhere else: on
a mother holding her child,
on a factory shut down,
the workers at home passing
through the paper. The stars
are here, each one on its own.
You can see where they may
still be. You could give names
to the constellations, ones for
this latest millennium: Dan the
Stockbroker, Sharon the
Newly Elected Official, Tim
the Self-Conscious. Everyone asleep
is drifting through a world
glimpsed during the day: slicing
a tomato, leading a meeting of
the zoning board, changing
stations on the car radio. Your
dogs are sleeping, too, of course,
one at the foot of the bed, the other
here beside you. If you woke them,
they would look up, lick your face,
then drop their great square heads
back down. You will stay
in the convenience of the dark,
maybe something outside listening in.

Traveling Back

After his wife's funeral,
he pulled his car off
the back road, stopped
beside Wilson Lake and
watched the fog over the
water. It was a place
he knew well, a place where
the fog always came, a tired,
good dog sleeping at his feet.
He wondered what
grief was and why
it sat in him like the
stars. She had been
an empty glass, summer,
a quilt at the end of the bed.
She had been the words
he never said. There
was no moon. The night
was a mute savant. He
wanted to fly. He
wanted to go home.

Selling the House

The buyers came to measure,
and we watched, trying
to drink coffee and continue
the card game. As they
stretched a tape along
the wall of family
photographs and along
the shelf cluttered with
shells and carved
Madonnas, we heard
her say, "I hate this
wall. I hope we can
put in a window." It
started to rain, and
the dog lay under
the table, and the
hummingbirds hovered
at the feeder while
the orioles pecked
at the orange halves
nailed along the porch
rail. In a week, it all
would go to sleep.
Under the maples,
birches, and pines.
Under the graves
of the dogs. Under

the rocks piled
every summer
along the shore.

Evensong

Tommy Kent, always sure about fixing
any engine. "Give me a day; I'll have it
back and running." Ben Cane, who hit
the high, hard one, his lonely strength
in pickup games. We'd try to pitch him
low and away. He'd wait. Draw a walk
or slice a double down the line. Days,
that's what there were: bordered, filled,
spread like a map with only the back
roads marked. If it rained, the world
was a porch, an attic if it snowed.
School was a lie insisting there were
things more serious than death.
Carol Lawson, amazing at math,
did calculus while we were sputtering
in the dust of algebra. Her breasts
were the first to come to class,
the first to fall away before she followed.
Every morning, I feed the dogs, carry
a bucket into the garden to deadhead.
Overnight, some blooms have browned
or wilted, lying across the stems that held.
I break them off but am never sure
about those that have faded and folded
in on themselves. Their centers do not
show, but the undersides take in the morning
light. And their names—cosmos, pansy,
cleome—feel happy on my tongue, never
stay the way Tommy, Ben, and Carol do.

Still Here

Easy world, you gave it once,
that quiet afternoon after
a morning rain. We
had lunch. Then, the sun
came out and we took
our sweat out into the
garden, pulled gently
on the weeds and lifted
the slugs off their path.
It was our own greenhouse,
lost under a wide sky, the
thunderheads now gone
on, the mud mixed
with the deep, muted
smell of leaves. That
was all, a morning
storm, a steamy afternoon,
a garden helping us
feel we belonged.

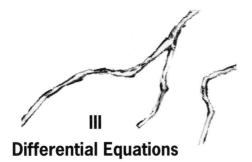

III
Differential Equations

Aubade for This Morning

The night was filled with rain,
lightning announcing our luck,
thunder rumbling its afterthought.
The dogs woke and quietly
came to the side of the bed.
The cat curled down between us.
Now in the damp of morning,
the leaves hold the early light
within each drop, the sun
rising into the sky's still
depth of cloud, across
the gray scrim of the day.
It is quiet, not silent—quiet
as the sparrows, finches,
and warblers singing through
the dripping branches,
their notes a not-quite-startling
welcome as we open the windows,
brew the coffee, let our breath
return to its steady wander.
My mother began her morning
saying, "Time for this day."
Today the lingering
of an old rain. The chill of 6 A.M.
The coffee. The musty smell
of crumbs, blankets, and pillows
on the daybed on the porch.

On Our Dog's Birthday

Throughout the day,
he'll press his wet nose
against the floor-to-ceiling
window and watch anything
that passes by, now and
then falling asleep. When
the cats come in, they'll
nuzzle their cold faces
against the soft warmth
of his forehead. We'll
also look into the day,
watch the thick gray
beech trees' branches
sway in the coming
winter storm. Today
our dog is ten. When
we go to another room,
he'll follow. When later
we take our walk, he will
wander off after smells
he finds along the way.
After we return, if I toss
his ragged stuffed lion,
he'll look at me, seem
to want to say, "You
don't have to play with me.
I'm fine," then mosey
over and take the toy

back to his spot. Tonight,
if he needs to go out, he
will sit by the side of the bed,
my wife and I sleeping deep
in our marriage, and woof
softly, clear his throat,
as if he doesn't want to be a bother.

Flying in over Key West

Maybe the clear water leads me to believe
coral is God's last hiding place.
But it's likely just the end of the highway,

the way US 1 stitches the islands
and tethers them to the bony finger
of the mainland. Something

makes me feel some of it will last—
a tin roof, the wood of a lobster trap,
bougainvillea winding through a wire fence.

The plane comes down across the haphazard flyway
of pelicans. An egret waits, motionless
beside a fishing boat rocking against a canal wall.

If you were here, we would go out tonight
and look for Key deer in the mangroves. We
would watch them trusting us, then go home.

Instead, once I hang up my shirts, I'll
go to Arnie's Seawater Shop and buy
you one of those pieces of pink coral,

the kind with a phony blue dolphin
rising up behind a seashell,
a bit of yellow glue showing along the edge.

Divine Women: The Woodblocks of Utamaro

Along the rock-shaved shore, they sit,
breasts dappled and open to the daylight.
Their red robes, slack across their salt-glistened backs,
hang above the rising tide, within the slow
arrival of rain. There is nothing
but silence, not a single word hovers near them.
They look down, lost in the language of waiting.

Miles out on the ocean's ineffable lift and toss,
the fishermen fling their weave of nets, stand
counterpoint in the roil, wait, then haul
in their catch, sort groundfish from eel
and feel the women taking them into the nothingness
of thrust and calm: alone, the night, time empty
as the lure of space between the stars.

Here the women know there is no hope.
They reach into the sea, let the intuition of fingers
feel for the abalone. When they cut one from its shell,
they imagine tasting its pink tongue of flesh,
the sea dripping from their hands, the salt
singeing their open palms. By their sides,
the weathered, brown wicker baskets soak
in the wet air. They will fill them in the only way
they know of being in the world. The wild young boy
who never leaves them, reaches above their robes
as if the moles on their breasts are stars.

The Rain on the Burren

I

The morning rain comes every day, bleak
across the grays of limestone. It falls
on the dolmen, austere and singular
since the cold people of the Stone Age
hoisted the great slab over their dead.
At home this rain would be a reason
to change our little plans. But here we
assume our noses will drip, our feet
will be wet as we walk the roadside
along the stone walls covered in gorse
and wild roses, our breath will warm
our hands. At home we would be
having our breakfast on the porch,
a bowl of strawberries in cold milk.
In this day's beginning we let our hands
wrap around a steaming cup of tea,
then find their way to each other.

II

The rain here is a burst along the horizontal
or a languid drizzle, the light seeming to lag
behind the day's gray crawl across the limestone.
Peat-dappled smoke rises sweet within the soft
damp, hints at a warm corner or, after the lost hours
of work, a hearth and finally sleep. The chill is mute.
Tomorrow the sun may come, glistening its light
across the subtleties of green and the blue

of the spring gentians, ellipses between the neolithic
slabs and glacial blunder of boulders. But always
this benevolence of stillness, the rain.

III

The rain falls as if it is God. It says Wellies,
raincoat, hood, and umbrella, says stay inside,
build the peat four stacks high, keep the tea water
boiling. We can do nothing about its whim,
its wind, and slash across the eyes. We
keep going to the window, a slant of hope
rising from our hearts' bog. We think of
daring a prayer against the blight, but
the rain is omnipotent and indifferent
as any deity. We simply say Amen.

IV

Our driver's face is weathered as the Burren.
"Thirty-five years a fisher, I was." His great
hands wrap around the steering wheel, and we
imagine them twisted into a full haul
of cod, crab, sole, and lobster. "I was
raised by me mother, nine of us was,
and never once did we buy a thing to eat.
Got it all from the earth, we did. Potatoes,
carrots, turnips, cabbages. Me uncle,
he bossed us and, oh, he was tough.
Had to be, you know; it bein' hard
work and us bein' kids and all." We
are going up into the hills near Doolin

to a castle for a night and a six-course meal.
We will look out to the Cliffs of Moher
over our venison, cheeses, wine, and
Bailey's cake. "We'd kill two pigs
for the year, and we had a tree
drippin' with pears. I'd walk up
to the castle where you be stayin'
and deliver the eggs, then climb to the top
and shoot the pigeons. It's where
they roosted. Still do, I'd imagine."
His hair is thick as gorse, his great
shoulders come round wider than the seat.
It's raining, the wind lifting whitecaps high
and far out on the Atlantic. He looks
toward the sea. "That's where I'd be," he says
setting down our bags. "You have a grand time,
and if you need another lift, just give me a shout."

V

The day the power went out across the Burren
the dogs lay down in the doorways of the pubs,
the cats curled up along the stone walls, and
the rain fell, gathered in the gutters, spilled
down the drainpipes. The yellow-gold
of the lichens, the purple in the rocks, the
blood-red of the geraniums lifted
their color as we walked the fields, let ourselves
soak into the late morning. "The power's gone out"
was the word along the fissures and villages.
"Don't know how long it will be." The gray
mass of cloud moved on the wind. The gorse

and hawthorn held the soft moss. We watched
for the feral goats to head toward the hilltop
while the sheep and cows grazed along the lowlands.

VI

Everyone's loneliness follows into the pub
like an old beggar, takes a stool at the bar,
and talks about how the clouds bring
shadows over the backs of the cows, how
the wind sends the rain slanting against
the windows. It pays for the pints, turns
its back to the television, asks what you did
today, if you're here by yourself, tells a joke
about the three priests who went fishing
after mass. At closing time, it takes the coaster
from under its glass, slips it into a pocket, says
see you tomorrow, walks out, head down, whistling.

VII

We shall leave behind the full Irish breakfast,
the clouds anonymous across the hills,
the rusting tractors clambering through the village
and along the lanes, and the "are ya now?" We'll
take home the soft, rolling walks along the greens,
the ways of talking in the gray of day and rock,
the index finger raised from the steering wheel
to say hello to anyone driving one's way. We
will remember the goodness of limestone,
cascading stream, and the cows lowing
in the pasturelands before another storm.

Walking the Creek with Dogs

"I do not think all dogs are angels. In fact, I don't think any are."
—Jeanne Schinto in *The Literary Dog*

Mine are, muddy
angels, slopping
their way ahead of me.
I watch my every step.
They head on, tails
wagging like assurances
that this is happiness.
Nothing in their heaven
is pure, just a twisting
creek, sand, rock,
rotting logs. Sometimes
they catch something
in the air's great mix
of scents, and they
veer, soaking, up
the bank, dripping
and sniffing into the
loosestrife, milkweed,
sassafras, and thistle.
I hear only the snap
of a stick and their soft
rustle through the mat
of grasses. Then they
are back, splashing
through the water,
stopping only to shake.

I slap at a deerfly,
feel August on my neck.
They carry their thick
coats on down the creek.

Setting out the Puzzle Pieces

When the long, slow quiet of lymphoma
filled my father's fingers, swelling them
into a day when he could no longer pull
the weeds from his gardens, he
set up the card table his mother had
played solitaire on and got out
a jigsaw puzzle, one with photos
of baseball legends—Gehrig, Cobb,
Pie Traynor, Hack Wilson, Musial,
Mathewson, Mel Ott. On the box's
cover, their cracked leather faces
floated over fat-fingered gloves,
barrel-handled bats, flat caps, baggy
knickers, and wide-stitched baseballs.
He dumped the pieces on the table,
put the cover back in the cupboard,
and turned over each piece, setting
the straight-edged ones off to the side.
I watched as he slowly wedged each
piece between his forefinger and thumb.

When he was seventeen and living
on the brick streets of Pittsburgh,
my father, a shortstop, was named
the best schoolboy player in the city
and, every time the Pirates had a day
game, took infield with the team.
Hall of Famer Honus Wagner, now

a coach, sat on the bench, stoic
as a steelworker. My father, nervous
as a supplicant, once dared to ask
him for advice. The great ghost
of a shortstop looked down, scraped
his spikes along the dugout floor,
and mumbled, "When the ball's hit at
you, catch it. Then throw it where you
should." My father wrapped his throwing
hand, callused from his father's tools,
around the fingers of his glove.

Yesterday I took the puzzle and dumped
the pieces. Turning them over one
by one, I felt my father's fingers
come alive in mine and remembered
how he'd slap a baseball at me,
skipping it off at a nasty angle
or short hopping it at my feet. He'd
say, "Watch it all the way into your glove."

The Gardeners

In the spring she
drops the seeds, he
covers them. He
digs up the weeds.
She cuts the flowers.
She takes the blooms
and puts them in
every room. They soar
red from the tables, sprout
yellow from the shelves,
hang purple from
the ceiling, blue
from the edges of
lampshades. Clusters
of flowers sit in
tiny pots on every
windowsill, in open
cupboards, behind
the sink. He stands
beside her as she tosses
all the wilted leaves
into a rusty bucket.
This house is heaven's
door, the air gathering
the bashful smells of
blossoms, roots, cut
stems, wet dirt, new
and rotting leaves.

My Father Gardening in Heaven

The flowers are no taller here.
The cosmos carry their saucers
of burgundy and white, the fuchsias
dangle their puckered blossoms
no farther down than they do on earth.
Every flower adds its promiscuity
of scent, its audacity of color
to the unencumbered hues of heaven.
My father imagines snow-on-the-mountain
spreading across the clouds, succulents
thriving in the fierce sunlight, bleeding
heart drooping in the perfect air. Here
there are no slugs peeling the leaves,
no aphids ravenous in a flower's veins.
The days are bereft of drought,
the nights solicit no unwelcome frost.
But my father, sleeping under the apple blossoms,
dreams of spider mites, leaf hoppers,
and lace bugs cutting across his every plant.
He wakes up shaking and reaching for a spray.
Adam turns from his hoeing, smiles. Eve
waves out the window. My father nods,
stands up, takes his rake and pulls it gently
over the straight and narrow furrows
he's loosened in the soft, sweet loam.

Raking Leaves with the Gods in July

For a month, there has been no rain.
Scattered over the pea stone paths

that lead us through the shade
of our gardens, beech and birch,

oak, ash, and even larch leaves
lie, their ends dry and curling

toward their veins. I rake and
make believe I am a Zen-traveled

monk smoothing the surface, quieting
the loss into a calm within a heart's

usual storm, the tines' slow scrape
assuming silence among the stones.

In the branches birds sing. The heat
is my Master saying, *Slow, slow.*

Move to the edge. The lack of rain
says, *Patience.* The gods say,

What is there to do? This, I say.
And? they say. *And this.* They

stand their rakes against a tree,
gather in the Adirondack chairs along

the narrowing stream. *But there is also
this,* I say, nodding toward the water.

A Few Days before Another Memorial Day Weekend

You think maybe if you screened in the porch.
You think fly fishing. You think rereading
Middlemarch or your grandmother's recipes.
There's summer ahead, lots of days, plenty
of pots to make a container garden: mounds
of begonias, asters, foxglove, cosmos, and coleus.
There's your sister's wedding, her third you think.
It will be small, huge, both; it doesn't matter.
And it does. It's not at all the same. What is
the same is your penmanship, no matter how many
calligraphy lessons or how hard you've tried
to change the way you cross your T's. What's
the same is birdsong and the taste of pepper. You
switch cereals, you turn off the television, the
back burner, the boss, the highway. There's a little
restaurant where you can order garlic mashed
potatoes and switch to blueberry pie. You think
if you throw away your shoes, buy a little car, a little
place in the country, make a little sense. You say yes
to four in the morning, yes to the dust on the table,
no to the days of the week, to wind chimes, number-two
lead pencils, the West Coast. You know there's
wax in your ears, there's time enough to tell, there's room
for it here—or even there. It's just that the dog is asleep
and the cats are asleep and the water is running, running
where your mother said it would run, running while
the welcome mat stays out. You wonder if you thought
of Buddha, but no one can think of Buddha. So you

think of Jesus thinking of Buddha, Jesus thinking of
Krishna thinking of Buddha who is not thinking, who is
letting the dream of a better kitchen wander off with the end
of a novel. No, you think of the nuthatch climbing down
the dead maple outside your bedroom window, you
think of the kid on the yellow bicycle, peddling like
mad, like crazy, like wildfire down the street.

Knowing Now You'll Never Be a Clown

But if you were, and if your grin
were painted red as a Coke can, a fire
engine, red as the Tabasco sauce
you spilled on your mother's carpet, and
if it lifted itself from the inside of one huge ear
to the other, and if your nose were a Ping-
Pong ball begging for a swipe, and if
your feet slept within white shoes, three feet long
and flapping, would you then be able to talk
to everything you really want to talk to: the
chickadees who come closer than your nieces,
that piece of paper blown across your lawn,
the rain, each nudge of green in your garden?
And when you put on your coat, that UN
of colors and scraps, that coat that would
make Joseph feel he had folded himself
into the pages of GQ, the one with the shoulders
rolling up to your cheeks, with buttons the size
of pancakes, and a hem like the border of
Czechoslovakia, would you want to walk
into church, quietly take your place with
the choir, and just as the minister finishes
the benediction, honk your horn? And
when you put on your polka-dotted tie, wide
as a summer afternoon, would you
want to pin the squirting yellow daisy
on your lapel, sit in the meeting,
and after the ayes have it, squeeze

the rubber bulb in your pocket? Then
again, maybe you would just stay home,
listen to jazz, the blues, or some swing,
open each of your cupboards and talk
about Tuesday or the way the light falls
across the counters, invite Lou Jacobs,
Emmett Kelly, Felix Adler, Otto Griebling,
hell, the whole clown alley, rent a calliope,
a center ring, one elephant, get out the pies,
and sit around waiting for a laugh.

Repairing the House

We'll learn the house can live
without our changes. We will

listen to its language. The cracks
along the stairway—they are sentences.

We will read what they say
when we go up, again when

we walk back down. When we
leave our sleep, our beds will hold

our place as the floor creaks under us.
If we fix the broken window, then

we will open it. The other windows
rise on their tracks; that's enough;

one staying shut, tight, will still bring
light for any day, the others the breeze.

And we will learn to be with the ivy
straying along the back brick walls,

twisting itself into the mortar, each spring
a chunk or two falling into the holly.

There is a draft under the porch door.
We could block the cold from sliding

toward our feet. Instead, we will wear
socks, ones you made, while we sit facing

each other, reading on the sofa, its stuffing
shifting under us, pillows giving way to what is left.

Sisley's "Snow at Louveciennes"

We see white on white, a woman
in the bleak center of the canvas,
this cold holding onto the rolling
snow lying along the fences,
tree limbs, hipped roofs,
stone walls of the lost village.
On a cottage door, a quiet blot
of blue. Wrapped in a tatter
of brown, the woman, deep
in the landscape's insistent flat,
has the anonymity of a still life.
She is your mother unable to return,
staring into the blizzard's dread
beauty, seeing only the sky,
a mute wash of blue hanging fragile,
spare as the frozen air. She stands
bordered by the indifference
of daylight, imagines a cardinal
cutting its wound across the snow,
a cat crawling under a cottage,
curling its tail around its sleep.

Instead of Vacationing in Maine

Here on our screened-in porch, the hot August
light falls like a shawl over the dogs, each asleep
in his bed, the big one stretched out in his long white

coat, the pup curled into a pile of pillows, one ear flopped
back over his forehead. The FM station sends "The
    Wasps"
into the humidity. Williams composed it at nineteen.

At nineteen I was lost. Cicadas stutter in the branches
    bending
over the stream drying now to a meandering line of cold
spring water that rises from the bottom of Kelly Lake

then twists for three miles before losing its trail into
the maw of Lake Michigan. Deer come, drink
from the creek then move closer, this year close

enough to gnaw the leaves from the mass of hostas
that surrounds the house. One kingfisher cackles back
and forth from branch to branch, pausing to peer down

for minnows, crayfish, and tadpoles. The gardens held
through July's dragging lack of rain. We helped,
sprinkling the pots with the watering can we found

years ago, its paint peeling and leaving a patina that
like a still life blends into the quieting hues of the scramble

of color: wine-red begonias, pale pink and purple

phlox, coleus, the pastels of daisy, gazania, the stunning
burgundy of bergamot, that seducer of hummingbird and
yellow jacket. In the late afternoon dragonflies pose

on the lilies' leaves, the day-mortal blooms leaning into
the sunlight as if to invite the swallowtails and monarchs.
All of this here, all of this leaving with the music and the
day.

The Comforting

A few words from Genesis, some
Duke Ellington, just the middle of the week.

Out in the yard, the anonymous robin; in
the neighbor's garden, a spray of poppies.

The configuration of nests: why mud, leaves,
string; why paper, sticks; why stones?

The lonely smell of a wet dog, the
way water stays in the world.

Your tongue, holding to the apple, tomato,
pear, letting go without your say.

Across the street, the oat grass turning yellow.

The Drywallers Listen to Sinatra while They Work

This morning, my mother, here
for the holidays, is washing
the breakfast dishes, when Al, wiry,
coated with drywall dust, takes
her hand and says, "I bet you loved
Sinatra. Dance?" The acrid smell
of plaster floats through the room.
Frank is singing, "All or Nothing
at All," and Al leads my mother
under the spinning ballroom lights
across the new subfloor. He
is smiling. She is looking over
his shoulder. The other guys
turn off their sanders. Al
and my mother move through
the dust, two kids back
together after the war. Sinatra
holds his last note. "It's been
seven years since I danced,"
my mother says. "Then
it was in the kitchen, too."
Al smiles again, says,
"C'mon then, Sweetheart!"
biting off his words like the ends
of the good cigars he carries
in his pocket. Sinatra's singing
"My Funny Valentine," and
my mother lays her hand in Al's.

110

They dance again, she looking
away when she catches my eye,
Al leading her back
across the layers of dust.

What We Do

In the distance the thunder
softly rumbles as we trim
back the basswood and
honeysuckle. A few drops
fall, the clouds hang
within the hollow air.
Our dog digs into the dirt,
lies down within the still
morning. We cut the peonies,
hoping the unopened buds
will hold against the downpour.
It's gotten darker.
We go to the porch, sit,
listen to the drops against
the trees' leaves, smell
the cool air coming up
from the garden's roots.

Waiting on the Beatitudes

For my father

You would be looking for something to do.
She would suggest cleaning the back bedroom.
You would head out to the gardens.

Sometimes when I look out the window,
I don't see you. The hawks hang over
the white pines. The heron stands

in the stream like a silent question.
There's no one there again. There's
no name left on the other side

of the stone wall. You lie close
to the indifference of grass.
Today a west wind lifts

the honeysuckle's leaves. I want
you to be washing your car, carrying
a load of leaf mulch out to your perennials,

watching the dark clouds, a house wren
tugging twists of straw from the bales
you stacked behind the cold frame.

The Man Who Wanted to Change the World

He thought changing the nouns
might help. No one could say
"gun" in the same old way. You
would have to pause, say,
"What's the name again? Oh,
yes, sassafras." You would hear,
"Give me the wisteria to the car,"
or find yourself asking, "Why
don't we add some whispers
to the bottom line?" He realized
this one long, hazy afternoon
while staring up into the trees,
into the wild acceptance
of their branches' tangle. He
watched the light settle on
the leaves. He believed
the robins, vireos, and
nuthatches could see it.
Later that evening, drying
his dinner plate, he felt everything
around him leaving, felt himself
alone amid the sparkles of dust.
Before bed, he addressed, sealed,
and stamped a stack of empty
envelopes, one for everyone
he loved. The next morning
he made his first list: bread dough,
lightning, salt, candle, mourning dove,

tunnel, while he thought of last laugh,
coffin, profit margin, knife,
proliferation, highway, fact.

Burying the Poems

The night is still, the leaves calm
as a corpse when the words tell me,
"Be like the poet Alexander Kutzenov.
Bury your poems." He sealed them
in glass jars like the finest currant jam,
laid them down into the earth and covered
their graves with leaves. I will do the same.
Slender light from the crawl of worms
will slide through the glass, lie between
the lines, along language's slow syntax.
The dreaming earth with its lost souls
of slug and beetle, ephemeral scat of cat
and dog, drifting scent of nosing possum,
raccoon, and deer will mulch the poems'
quiet stay, the rhythms alkaline, the meanings
dormant in their disfigured corms. Moles
will come, nuzzle each jar. Voles will spin
like dervishes around the lids. Winter will
bring the hard frost tightening the ground.
Then following the breakage of spring and
the blisters of summer, the fall will raise
no harvest. Nothing there. Nothing to be there.
Only the jars under the lost dark green of leaves.

Keeping On

But of course he couldn't decide.
One thing always led to another.
Like the way the lady drove down the street.
No, more like the way the dog . . .
Well, whatever it was, it was
not nearly as traumatic as the way
the man two blocks over . . .
or was it yesterday's mail? He was
lost, or so it seemed, until he learned
to plant onions amid the hollyhocks
and realized that sticking spoons
in one part of the garden attracted moonlight
long after the flowers had faded. And so,
he bought a hundred more spoons and
arranged them throughout the flowers.
He watered them. And watched them
stay the same. And let them
take the moonlight. One day he realized
he'd forgotten about the lady
and the way the dog and the man two blocks
over and the mail. He found himself
smiling as he sprinkled the spoons.

Living in the Twenty-First Century

Long before there was this day
another day came. Maybe it rained
or there was a little sunlight. People

got up and did what they always do.
Birds sang and the cats wanted out,
or in. You and I weren't here,

but the world didn't know. Trees
grew and nobody noticed. Someone
was cruel. Someone else

tried not to be. Maybe the weather
shifted unexpectedly and plans
had to be changed. This morning

we watched our day begin. We
wondered if it would be good,
wondered if it would rain.

Acknowledgments

Special thanks to Myra Kohsel for her patience and help in the assembly of the manuscript.

The author is grateful for his students and to Hope College for support, without which the completion of many of these poems would have been much more difficult.

Credits

Several of these poems appeared, some in a different form, in the following journals. I am grateful to the editors and staffs of each:

Artful Dodge
Cairn
Controlled Burn
Crab Orchard Review
Dogwood
The Driftwood Review
Evansville Review
Free Lunch
FIELD
5 AM
The Georgia Review
Gloss
The Griffin
Gulf Coast
Harpur Palate
*How To Be This Man: The Walter Pavlich Memorial
  Poetry Anthology*
The Journal
The Listening Eye
LIT
Louisville Review
The Mid-America Poetry Review

Passages North
Pebble Lake Review
Poems from the Third Coast: Contemporary Michigan
  Poetry (Wayne State University Press)
Poet Lore
Poetry
Poetry East
Prairie Schooner
Rattapallax
Re)Verb
Runes
Southern California Anthology: USC
Southern Indiana Review
The Texas Observer
Voices Along the River
West Wind Review

"The Dry Wallers Listen to Sinatra while They Work" received first prize in the Say the Word Poetry Competition sponsored by the Ellipse Art Center in Arlington, Virginia, and *Poet Lore.* David St. John, judge.

"The History of the Pencil" was selected as runner-up for the Ann Stanford Prize from the University of Southern California. Dana Gioia, judge.

Some of these poems were previously published in *Against Elegies,* which was chosen by Sharon Dolin and Billy Collins for the 2001 Chapbook Award from the Center for Book Arts, New York City.

122